A SERIES FOR THE
AMERICAS

A SERIES FOR THE AMERICAS

WOODFORD PRESS
660 Market Street, San Francisco, CA 94104
Visit our website at www.woodfordpub.com
Book design by Laurence J. Hyman

Produced in partnership with and licensed by
MAJOR LEAGUE BASEBALL PROPERTIES, INC.

A Series For The Americas is an official publication of Major League Baseball

To order additional copies of this, or any other *Official Book of the World Series,* or for a Woodford Press catalog, please call toll-free, 1-888-USA-BOOK, or 415-397-1853

Simultaneously printed in Spanish

ISBN: 0-942627-33-8
First Printing: November 1997
Printed and bound in the United States of America
Distributed to the trade by National Book Network, Lanham, MD

A SERIES FOR THE AMERICAS

By Bruce Jenkins

The 1997 World Series moved through South Florida like a warm, cleansing breeze. It arrived to the sounds of salsa music, the scent of rich Cuban cigars and the sight of many nationalities united as one. It said farewell through the joy and tears of the Florida Marlins, a championship team as unlikely as it was fascinating.

The Marlins won this one for Manager Jim Leyland, the crusty baseball lifer who celebrated his first title with childlike exuberance. They won it for veterans like Bobby Bonilla and Gary Sheffield, and for future stars like Charles Johnson and Edgar Renteria. They won it in just their fifth year of existence, against a Cleveland franchise that dates, in various forms, back to 1869. But more than anything, these teams staged a championship for Latin America. On the grand tropical stage of Miami, melting pot for Hispanic cultures, the World Series offered untold inspiration in countries around the world.

They felt it in Colombia, Venezuela, Puerto Rico and the Dominican Republic. They cherished it in Little Havana, center of Miami's teeming Cuban population, when a 22-year-old defector named Livan Hernandez became the most decorated ballplayer of October. And in the back rooms and secret hideaways of Fidel Castro's Cuba, there was a bittersweet sense of pride and satisfaction, a reminder of the days when Luis Tiant, Tony Perez, Camilo Pascual, Bert "Campy" Campaneris and Zoilo Versalles graced the World Series landscape.

To a degree, there was precedent for such international influence. The 1962 San Francisco Giants, featuring Juan Marichal, Orlando Cepeda, Jose Pagan and two of the Alou brothers (Felipe and Matty) were the first World Series team with a heavily Hispanic flavor. In their wake came the Big Red Machine, the great Oakland teams of the early 1970s, the unforgettable performances of Roberto Clemente and the frenzy surrounding Fernando Valenzuela in 1981. But Latin America had never seen anything like October 1997. As the Series progressed, it was difficult to find a standout player who was *not* Hispanic.

For the Indians, there was shortstop Omar Vizquel, right fielder Manny Ramirez, relief pitcher Jose Mesa, second baseman Tony Fernandez and the remarkable Sandy Alomar, who put his name alongside Johnny Bench, Yogi Berra and the other great catchers of Post Season lore. The Marlins had Renteria, whose clutch single won Game 7; left fielder Moises Alou, who hit .348 with three homers and 15 RBI; Bobby Bonilla, whose baserunning and seventh-game homer overshdowed a .167 batting average; relief pitchers Felix Heredia and Antonio Alfonseca, who combined for $10\,^1/_3$ scoreless innings; pitcher Alex Fernandez, out with an arm injury but a vibrant dugout presence, and Hernandez, voted Most Valuable Player of both the NLCS and the World Series.

This was truly a series for the world, a series crossing oceans and language barriers and finding its way into dusty, poverty-stricken towns where the power of soccer had never been challenged. A record audience watched on television in 205 countries, and some 40 million people tuned into the 365-

station Latin Broadcasting Company radio network. Just as American kids' lives changed forever in the 1950s and 1960s, catching the heroics of Mantle, Mazeroski and Koufax during a grade-school recess, there were stories like the one out of Colombia, where an evening soccer match featuring an immensely popular club was moved to 4 p.m. so it wouldn't conflict with the baseball broadcast.

And for those with a sentimentalist's heart, there was one small triumph for international harmony. When the Series started, Livan Hernandez' mother was at home in Cuba, looking for a place where she might be able to hear a static-ridden radio signal. But on the night of Game 7, Miriam Carreras was sitting in a luxury suite at Pro Player Stadium, watching her son's team win it all. ``I love you, Miami!'' he kept shouting — some of the first words anyone could recall him speaking in English — and the feeling was mutual.

Hernandez wasn't even in the Marlins' rotation when they opened the Division Series against San Francisco. But he got nationwide attention with a riveting, four-inning relief performance in Game 2, and in Game 5 of the NLCS against Atlanta, he personally altered the balance of power in the National League. Hernandez went the distance that day, striking out 15 in a 2-1 victory that gave Florida a 3-2 series lead.

The Marlins still had to finish the job. The Braves had been down 3-1 to the St. Louis Cardinals in 1996 before taking their familiar place in the World Series. But they were no match for the talent — or the determination — of Kevin Brown. In a riveting seventh-inning scene, Brown went face-to-face with Leyland in the Marlins' dugout and delivered a stern, impassioned lecture, insisting that he finish what he started. Leyland relented, and Brown's complete-game performance sent the Braves home for the winter. On the final play, a force-play toss from second baseman Craig Counsell, Renteria cheerfully caught the ball without the use

of his glove. It was a moment that captured the Marlins' raw, street-tough nature, and when you think about it, Renteria was probably the first man in history to clinch a trip to the World Series with his bare hand.

The Indians' road through October was longer, more arduous, and at times, unbelievable. The sturdy presence of rookie pitcher Jaret Wright carried them through the Division Series against the Yankees, who were never the same after Alomar's stunning home run off Mariano Rivera with the Indians down to their last four outs in Game 4. The American League Championship Series, against the Baltimore Orioles, was one for the ages. It was stranger than fiction — and more compelling, too, as long as you weren't Lenny Webster.

Game 3 began with a magnificent pitching duel between Orel Hershiser and Baltimore's Mike Mussina in the gorgeous late-afternoon light of Jacobs Field. Some five hours later, their names were only vaguely familiar. Ten relief pitchers had come and gone. Marquis Grissom was dancing off third base in the bottom of the 12th inning as Vizquel steeled himself for a squeeze bunt. He fanned. The ball kicked free. Grissom sprinted home with the game-winning run as Webster, thinking Vizquel had fouled it off, made no real effort to make the tag. The game has seen some bizarre finishes in the Post Season, but this was a first: A botched bunt turning into sudden victory.

The aftermath tormented Webster, but he was only beginning to get acquainted with a little patch of dirt they called the ``Cuyahoga Triangle.'' In the fifth inning of Game 4 the following night, Arthur Rhodes threw a wild pitch that evaded Webster, came to rest no more than 20 feet from home plate — and scored *two* Cleveland runs, the signature play in a game finally decided by Alomar's single in the bottom of the ninth.

The Indians hit just .193 in this series. They struck out a playoff-record 62 times. But they were starting to believe that strange, mysterious forces were at work, and Game 6 offered some hearty evidence. During batting practice at Camden Yards, starting second baseman Bip Roberts was struck on the left thumb by a sharply hit ball. It came off the bat of Tony Fernandez, who took Roberts' place in the lineup. And it was Fernandez who hit the 11th-inning homer off Armando Benitez that gave Cleveland the pennant. ``I feel it in my veins,'' Fernandez said afterward. ``I believe that God has given us the World Series.''

To be sure, the Series never felt like this. From the gently falling snow of Cleveland to the sensuous humidity of Miami, there was a contrast unprecedented in the game's long history. But the differences went well beyond the weather. The Indians were named after a Penobscot Indian who, in 1897, became the first Native American to play in the big leagues. The original Marlins included Jeff Conine, who still plays for the team, still enjoying the prime of life.

When the Marlins reminisce, they go all the way back to

1992 — the tales of Charlie Hough and Orestes Destrade and the wacky night their team hotel was overrun by a convention of bagpipers. The Indians are the franchise of Nap Lajoie, Addie Joss and Cy Young, superstars before World War I. A franchise with just three World Series appearances — 1920, 1948 and 1954 — before the advent of Jacobs Field changed everything. The Cleveland fan knows that the last world title came in 1948, and that Satchel Paige pitched in that Series. The Cleveland fan remembers a 34-year spell (1960-93) when the team never finished higher than fourth. He knows Max Alvis, Barry Latman and Joe Lis, just as he knows Boudreau, Feller and Wynn. He knows that Vada Pinson, Roger Maris, Johnny Vander Meer and Pistol Pete Reiser all passed through Cleveland, and that Billy Martin and Jim Piersall both played on the 1959 team. The Cleveland fan gets the full meaning of Trader Lane, Sudden Sam, ``Veeck as in Wreck'' and ``Don't Knock the Rock'' without hearing the details, and he knows that there is no inherent reward for patience, passion or suffering. Even with two World Series in the past three years, the Indians have found heartbreak at the finish line.

This time, of all places, it happened in the tropics.

Game 1 in Miami was a trip into exotic new territory, the province of pink stucco, blue neon and the orange-gray clouds of a captivating sunset. Visitors got the sense of an autumnal vacation as they lay on the beach, savored the intoxicating scent of post-rainstorm humidity, stepped into air-conditioned hotel lobbies to the soothing sound of a flamenco guitar. The perimeter of Pro Player Stadium was a dizzying swirl of musical flavor, from salsa bands to Brazilian drumbeats to rattling maracas. It seemed more a festival than a sporting event; faces in the crowd included Tiger Woods, Joe DiMaggio, Kevin Costner and Gloria Estefan. The massive blue tarpaulin was removed from the upper deck — a place generally occupied only by football fans — and the attendance of 67,245 was the World Series' largest in 34 years. The fans, estimated to be roughly 30 percent Hispanic, waved the colorful flags of a half-dozen countries.

``We've got a thousand things dividing us,'' wrote Dan Le Batard in the *Miami Herald*. ``But the Marlins have moved through us like an electric current, fusing us. When the people start chanting players' names, it's one of the few times you'll hear South Florida speaking with one voice.''

That voice was unmistakable. In the words of one Puerto Rican restaurant owner in Little Havana, ``Livan's pitching. Alou hits. Every time they slam the ball, it's like the game speaks in Spanish.''

This wasn't a chilly night in Baltimore, a roof-covered evening in Toronto or even a sun-kissed afternoon in Los Angeles; this was something entirely different. ``You always think the Dodgers and Yankees, apple pie and history,'' said the Indians' Orel Hershiser. ``But this is a different kind of World Series. I welcome the humidity and the 80 degrees. We're writing history instead of reliving it.''

It seemed entirely appropriate that Hernandez, the intriguing young pitcher out of Cuba, would start the opener. He pitched 5 2/3 innings for the win in a 7-4 victory, spiced by consecutive home runs off the bats of Alou and Charles Johnson off Hershiser in the fourth inning. Johnson's towering shot into the upper deck was particularly awe-inspiring, certainly one of the great tape-measure blasts of modern Series history (joining Reggie Jackson's shots in 1977

and 1978 and an upper-deck homer by Baltimore's Eddie Murray in the 1983 finale at Philadelphia). In the category of back-to-back homers, there was more exclusive company: Alou and Johnson joined the likes of Babe Ruth-Lou Gehrig, Roger Maris-Mickey Mantle and Frank Robinson-Brooks Robinson in World Series history.

Robb Nen, the Marlins' flame-throwing short reliever, was totally overpowering at the finish. The Marlins' speed gun showed readings of 101 and 102 mph as Nen struck out Jim Thome in the ninth inning, and while some questioned the validity of such figures, there was no doubting Nen's intimidation. ``I don't know how you do that,'' said teammate Darren Daulton. "And I don't know how you hit that."

The Marlins were looking to gain a two-game edge behind the formidable Brown, who hadn't lost since July 27, but Vizquel set an ominous tone with his one-out double in the first inning and David Justice's single gave Cleveland a quick 1-0 lead. Brown seldom looked sharp, giving up a two-run, sixth-inning homer to Alomar, and by the conclusion of the Indians' 6-1 win, Chad Ogea had established himself as the night's dominant pitcher. In a tribute to the resiliency of the Indians' pitching staff, Ogea, Wright and rookie left-hander Brian Anderson became centerpiece figures after a season that landed eight Cleveland pitchers (including Jack McDowell and John Smiley) on the disabled list. Ogea earned his World Series start with a strong September, and his 6 2/3-inning performance squared the series as it headed back to Cleveland.

For Leyland, this was a trip back home. He comes from the Toledo suburb of Perrysburg, Ohio, a place where they still call him ``Jimbo'' and remember his days as a three-sport star in high school. Leyland wasn't just a leader (quarterback, point guard, catcher). He was the kind of kid who would beg his coach for a reprieve from study hall so he could prepare a muddy baseball field after a morning rainstorm. The kid who

it's the pulsating atmosphere in the stands. Opposing players mentioned it constantly during the Post Season, saying they'd never seen anything like it. ``This is the kind of place where you talk about the `tenth man' and really mean it,'' said Indians pitcher Charles Nagy. ``The people here are unbelievable. I think they've played a huge part in our playoff wins. They just scream and yell the whole time. You feed off that.''

They were loud, they were well-behaved, and like the Indians' players, many of them wore red socks up to their knees. They certainly needed every bit of warm clothing for Game 3, a night where the wind-chill fell to 23 degrees by the middle innings. But even the throaty passion of these loyal fans couldn't forestall the Marlins' 14-11 win.

This game was an awakening for Gary Sheffield, who had spent much of the Post Season watching ``ball four'' sail high and away. One of the most feared hitters in the game, his swing a savage bolt of lightning, Sheffield was beginning to wonder ``if anyone would ever pitch to me.'' It happened in the wintry Game 3, Sheffield producing a solo homer in the first, a seventh-inning double that tied the game, 7-7, and a two-run single during Florida's seven-run rally in the ninth. Sheffield also made a spectacular defensive play in right field, climbing the wall to haul down Jim Thome's bid for an extra-base hit.

The lasting memory, however, was of something far more subtle. It was the simple act of Bobby Bonilla hustling from first base to third on a bad wheel.

Bonilla's tender left hamstring was becoming a popular story line of the Series, and it wasn't reading his way. There were reports that Bonilla, adamantly against playing as a designated hitter, had talked Leyland into letting him play third base for the entire Series — as long as he could walk. The notion left much to be desired in the early innings as Bonilla made two errors and grounded into a double play

routinely broke into the local gymnasium for late-night basketball sessions — and when a policeman showed up, he'd shoot with Leyland for a half-hour or so before chasing him out. Jim's oldest brother is the Rev. Thomas J. Leyland, pastor of a 135-year-old Catholic Church (Father Leyland has a Marlins' hat rack in his office). And this was a particularly special time for Leyland's 85-year-old mother, Veronica, who still lives in the five-bedroom house where Jimbo grew up. In a lovely moment, Leyland sent her by limousine to Jacobs Field, where she spent a long, chilly evening watching happily from the stands.

``You know, the first ballgame I ever saw was in Cleveland, the old Municipal Stadium,'' said Leyland. ``It was the summer of '54. Mike Garcia and Early Wynn were on the mound. The Indians won a doubleheader against the White Sox, and Larry Doby hit a home run. I'll never forget my dad taking me to that game.''

The modern-day scene at Jacobs Field is quite unforgettable, probably unmatched in all of baseball. The ballpark and downtown Cleveland have grown as one, transforming a bleak, downtrodden area into a thriving neighborhood upon the stadium's opening in 1994. The revitalization has seen the arrival of 31 new business establishments within two blocks of second base, with plans for much more, and wherever you are — Camden Yards, Coors Field, Fenway Park — there's nothing like the sight of thousands of fans streaming through town on their way to the ballpark.

``Visiting clubs used to come to Cleveland and never get a taste of it,'' says manager Mike Hargrove. ``You could go downtown on a Sunday night, shoot a cannonball down the street and not hit anybody. Now fans come downtown for the game and they stay, for the restaurants and everything else — and they come back.''

If there's one thing that separates Cleveland from the rest,

three playoff series, all of them personal disappointments. He put his head down and went for broke.

``He hesitated for just a second,'' said Leyland. ``Too long, to be honest. Then it's like he had a flash — this is the World Series — and he went.''

He went, and he scored. A strong throw from Marquis Grissom struck the sliding Bonilla on the arm, and when the ball caromed toward the stands, Bonilla cruised home with the tiebreaking run. ``It's the World Series,'' said Conine. ``Your body does things that your mind might not agree with. You never know if you'll get back here again.''

Grissom was left with the history books, having hit safely in his 15th consecutive World Series game. The streak ended there, two short of Hank Bauer's record (with the Yankees of the late 1950s), but Grissom moved past Clemente, who had the distinction of playing in 14 Series games and hitting safely in all of them.

When Game 4 arrived the following night, it wasn't just colder at Jacobs Field. The teams endured intermittent snow, 35-degree weather and a 15-degree wind chill in the coldest World Series game ever played. The Series hadn't seen anything like this since 1979, when they postponed Game 1 due to a blanket of snow in Baltimore.

Cleveland won the survival test, 10-3, behind the combined six-hit pitching of Wright and Anderson. Alomar continued his postseason rampage with two singles, a double and three RBI. Williams, who hit .385 in the Series and played a marvelous third base, cracked a two-run homer in the eighth. And the players from both teams attacked the conditions with a warrior-like mentality, backing off excuses, just blowing on their hands and persevering as little flecks of snow fell from the sky.

``This is what we play for,'' said Alomar. ``This is where everybody wants to be. You go from 80-degree weather to 30-degree weather and it's tough, but if that's how it will be, then let it snow.''

The Series hadn't been a particularly memorable one to this point. It had been witness to earnest criticism, including some scathing commentary from Leyland (on the late starting times and complaints about the Marlins as a wild-card entry) and Acting Commissioner Bud Selig (on the excessive length of games). Everyone seemed a little bit cranky, for one reason or another. But Game 5, an 8-7 Marlins victory in significantly milder weather, signaled a change.

While sloppy at times, the game had a stirring ebb and flow. Alomar and Alou traded three-run homers as the Series' Latin flavor kicked into high gear. Alou's ninth-inning single scored a run that proved to be vital, as the Indians fell just short with a three-run rally. Nen stared down Alomar for the game's final out, a fly ball deep to Sheffield in right. And if there were any doubts about Livan Hernandez's talent or mental resolve, they were thoroughly erased on the season's final night in Cleveland. Hernandez allowed five earned runs, walked eight and threw 147 pitches, but he went eight innings and became the first rookie in 50 years (since the Yankees' Spec Shea in 1947) to win two World Series starts.

``Livan wasn't rattled. He never is,'' said Alex Fernandez, a Miami-raised Cuban. ``This is not pressure for him. To get out of Cuba the way he had to do it, and deal with all that came after — that's pressure.''

with the bases loaded, hobbling badly on his way to first base.

``You have to understand the relationship these guys have,'' said Marlins third-base coach Rich Donnelly, who goes back to the Pittsburgh days with both Leyland and Bonilla. ``Jim gets annoyed at things Bobby does or says, but deep down, he loves him. If all the husbands and wives understood each other the way these guys do, there would be no such thing as divorce.''

When the sixth inning arrived, everything changed. With a national-TV audience cringing at Bonilla's every move, he suddenly made a backhanded stop of Matt Williams' sharp grounder down the third-base line, then uncorked a perfect throw from his knees. He *had* to make that play; a third error would have been intolerable. Properly energized, Bonilla was about to turn the entire game around.

With the game tied at 7-7, Bonilla led off the ninth with a walk. Daulton followed with a bullet single to right-center off Eric Plunk, and a reasonable man — especially one with a limp — would have stopped at second. But Bonilla had waited 11 years to play in the World Series. He had endured

With the gravity of his Post Season effort gaining full impact, Hernandez was recalling other great rookies of the World Series: Jackie Robinson, Fred Lynn, Mike Boddicker, the Indians' own Duster Mails and Gene Bearden, the 1996 performances of Derek Jeter and Andruw Jones. How loose was Hernandez, how self-assured? As he approached the mound for the first inning, a funk number thundering through the stadium public-address system, he did a little hip-swiveling dance.

``I think Livan's in a little world of his own, to be honest with you,'' said Leyland, ``and that's good. I think he has respect, but I don't think he has fear. This is a very tough kid. I don't think anything's going to shock him.''

The saga of Hernandez's mother was now gaining momentum. On the eve of the Series, she had been issued an emergency visa by U.S. officials, but her plans to visit Miami got tangled in the red tape of Cuban-government approval. Livan has ceased to exist in the eyes of the state-controlled media — broadcasts of American baseball are routinely scrambled in Cuba — and Miriam Carreras traveled to Havana from her home on Isla de la Juventud, nearly 100 miles to the south, to experience his Game 1 start in some way. At a private home, she and her friends gathered around a radio, struggling to pick up a faint signal from a Spanish-language station in Miami. Reports had them moving a makeshift antenna, a straightened-out clothes hanger, to get better reception. At one point, the woman of the house asked her young grandson to stand a little closer to the set, hoping that might help.

Suddenly, on the night of Game 5, there was a breakthrough. Because Hernandez was pitching, Radio Marti — the U.S. government's broadcast system out of Miami — picked up the Spanish-speaking play-by-play for nationwide Cuban broadcast. A clear signal was coming into Cuba for the first time in memory. Meanwhile, reports out of Havana indicated that fans were migrating to certain hotels and beach towns where a television signal could be picked up by satellite. After his Game 5 victory, Hernandez indicated that his mother might have been among the fortunate. ``She was watching,'' he said through an interpreter. When asked about the details, he said, ``It's a secret.''

Miriam Carreras' journey was almost complete. On the afternoon of Game 7, she arrived from Cuba — her visa finally intact — and saw Livan for the first time in two years. The Series had returned to Miami, complete with 80-degree weather, sunlit skies and the billowing flags of many nations. It all seemed perfect: Just one win from the championship, Kevin Brown on the hill. And the Game 6 hero would be . . .

Chad Ogea? Again?

Ogea outdid himself this time. Aside from allowing just one run in five innings for his second win of the Series, Ogea shocked Brown with a two-run single in the second inning and a crisp double down the right-field line in the fifth. Until this night, Ogea was hitless in his big-league career (0-for-5). ``For my last hit,'' he said, ``you've got to go back to my senior year in high school.'' But he's always fancied himself a hitter, going back to his childhood on the Louisiana bayou when his father taught him the art. All he needed was the right bat.

``I put away the bat they gave me with the World Series logo on it, and I borrowed one from Hershiser,'' said Ogea. ``Orel's bat was fine. He's a pretty good hitter.''

The stage was now set for Game 7, one that would take its place among the most memorable of the past: Enos Slaughter scoring from first base in 1946; Sandy Amoros' catch in 1955; Mazeroski's homer in 1960; McCovey's line drive settling into Richardson's glove in 1962; the great Smoltz-Morris pitching duel in 1991. Throughout October there had been a revival of baseball interest, disgruntled fans embracing it once again, finding the game was simply too good to ignore. If there were any skeptics left, Game 7 had all the answers.

Once again, veteran second baseman Tony Fernandez was linked to Indians history in ways more critical than anyone thought possible. He had won the pennant with that unlikely home run at Camden Yards. Now he was stroking a two-run single off Al Leiter in the third, and through eight innings, Florida's only answer was Bonilla's solo homer in the seventh. The Indians had received a brilliant 6 2/3 innings from Wright, they had a 2-1 lead going into the ninth, and they had ace reliever Jose Mesa trying to close it out. Just three more outs, and the 49-year wait would be over.

Down in the Marlins' dugout, Leyland felt the weight of his 33-year baseball career bearing down on him. By the age of 26, he was through as a player. He spent years enduring the creaky buses, bumpy fields and poorly lit ballparks of the Minor Leagues. He had come to represent the personification of big-league heartbreak, having lost three torturous National League Championship Series as manager of the Pittsburgh Pirates. Mention Leyland's name and the flashback was on, right back to that fateful night in Atlanta, Sid Bream sliding home safely on Francisco Cabrera's single to left.

Things felt different this time. Leyland was in the home dugout, the air was thick and sultry, and his Marlins had

Nagy in favor of Wright, son of former big-league pitcher Clyde Wright, because he loved the kid's style and panache. Now, with Mesa coming up short, he was asking Nagy to save the World Series.

``I wouldn't say I was angry,'' said Nagy. ``It was just such an uncomfortable situation. That's something I've never had to do.''

Nagy escaped a tense, two-on crisis by retiring Alou to end the 10th, but Bonilla opened the 11th with a single to right. Counsell sent a one-out grounder to Fernandez — there's that irrepressible figure again — and in a horrible moment of indecision, wondering if he might have a force on Bonilla at second, Fernandez let the ball slip into right field for an error. With runners at first and third, an intentional walk to Jim Eisenreich loaded the bases.

Nagy now dealt with Devon White. He hit a grounder to second base and there was bellowing, shouting, outright screaming from the stands, a moment of excruciating tension. Fernandez, gathering himself, calmly fired home to nail Bonilla for the second out.

It was so fitting, in the series for Latin America, that Renteria came to the plate. Back home in Barranquilla, Colombia, life had changed irrevocably. New baseball fans were sprouting daily; the family home became *the* place to watch the Series. That little town became a symbol for the game's global popularity, and for Renteria, there would be no judgement. He would return home a hero, win or lose.

The pitch was a breaking ball, down and away. Renteria stands up to the plate like Sheffield, furiously wiggling his bat in an endearing imitation of his teammate's style, but he plays for moments exactly like this, where a crisp single up the middle wins the game. Seven times already this season, Renteria had ended ballgames in Miami. Now he was timing the pitch perfectly, sending it right back toward Nagy, who made only the slightest contact with a frantic lunge of his glove. The ball rolled into center field, Counsell leaped onto home plate with the winning run, and the Marlins had their championship.

For the players, the middle-of-the-diamond pileup was an instinctive reaction. They simply went crazy, all as one. Leyland didn't quite know how to act. Not at first. After all those years, all the cigarettes and coffee and overnight stays in his ballpark office because he was too damn tired to move, he had to figure someone else wins the title. But now it was his.

``If we win this game tonight,'' Leyland confided to reporters before the game, ``I'll show you how I enjoy it.'' He showed them, all right. The Marlins had just won their championship faster than any expansion team in history — five years to the Mets' eight — but suddenly the World Series was about just one man, one story. Jim Leyland took a victory lap around the stadium, waving and smiling and pumping his fists, and his players savored it like adoring sons. Bonilla, Sheffield, Hernandez, one by one they grabbed their manager for a long, heartfelt embrace.

``I guess you get crazy when things like this happen,'' said Leyland. ``I've made an ass of myself more than once in my life, and I probably did tonight. But my wife is with me. I think she'll excuse me.''

Leyland was excused by everyone who ever cared

made a habit out of victories (28) in their last at-bats. Before the game he told his team in the locker room, ``When you come back here, you will be world champions.'' And he truly believed it. He was about to discover why.

At a time when a solo home run would tie the game, the Marlins played it much smarter. Alou cleverly poked a leadoff single to center field, casting a look of nausea across Hargrove's face in the Cleveland dugout. Mesa struck out Bonilla, but Charles Johnson executed a brilliant slice of situational hitting, drilling an opposite-field single that sent Alou to third. Counsell, the little second baseman who had been languishing in the Colorado Rockies' system only months before, hit a searing line drive to right field that became the game-tying sacrifice fly. Game 7 would go to extra innings.

The Marlins' bullpen had become unhittable. Alfonseca, Heredia, Dennis Cook, Nen, Jay Powell — together they pitched two-hit shutout relief over the last five innings. For Hargrove, it was a time of desperation. He had shunned

Team Of The Americas

about baseball. For all we know, he might still be celebrating. They said he danced like a champ as the Marlins' celebration raged on that Sunday night, and at a victory celebration on Tuesday, Leyland approached the microphone at Pro Player Stadium and sent the crowd into hysterics by yelling a very James Brown-like, ``I feel good!''

They're still talking about the big parade in South Florida that day, how the team traveled so effortlessly from downtown to Little Havana and up to Fort Lauderdale in an all-day party, how ethnic friction was put aside as black, white and Latin fans rallied behind a common cause. For Latin America in its finest baseball moment, the 1997 World Series was surely a glimpse into the future. As for the game in its birthplace, a very familiar story was told. Every quibble and complaint just disappeared, as if by magic, lost in the beauty of pure October baseball. It always wins in the end.

Miami, Florida   Oct. 18, 1997

GAME/JUEGO 1

The largest crowd to watch a World Series game in more than three decades, 67,245, witnessed an exciting Game 1 victory for the home team. Powered by Moises Alou's three-run homer off the left-field foul pole in the fourth inning, the victorious Marlins, who had reached the World Series faster than any expansion team in Major League Baseball history, jumped on Indians starter Orel Hershiser for seven earned runs and took the game, 7-4. Twenty-two-year-old Cuban rookie Livan Hernandez, Florida's playoff pitching hero, gave the game an international flavor that would be highlighted throughout the Series.

Gloria Estefan

Marlins mania reached its zenith as Cuban-born Livan Hernandez delivered the first pitch (opposite). The 22-year-old rookie, who took Miami native Alex Fernandez's spot in the starting rotation, won the game despite allowing three runs and eight hits in $5\,^2/_3$ innings. Left: the two managers meet.

"This is a tremendous dream, pitching in the World Series. It's the maximum."
— Livan Hernandez

"*The roar of the Marlins was deafening. All baseball heard it, this expansion team hurtling toward the World Series with the impudence and impatience of youth.*"
—Gregg Doyel, in the *Miami Herald*

*"Now that I'm older, I
have to show the passion."*
—Orel Hershiser

Bip Roberts (opposite, top left)
had two doubles and scored a
run in Game 1. David Justice
(opposite, top right), playing in
his fourth World Series,
contributed two hits. Veteran
Orel Hershiser (above)
struggled, giving up six hits and
seven runs in 4 $\frac{1}{3}$ innings.
Florida's Craig Counsell (right)
slides into third base in the
third. He eventually scored on
Gary Sheffield's ground out.

Moises Alou's three-run homer in the fourth gave the Marlins a 4-1 lead. Catcher Charles Johnson (opposite) followed Alou with a solo home run to give Florida a 5-1 advantage.

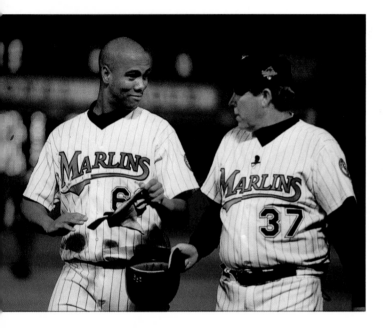

"I wouldn't recommend to another team to lose the first game of a series—it's just not good for your mental health at all."

—Mike Hargrove

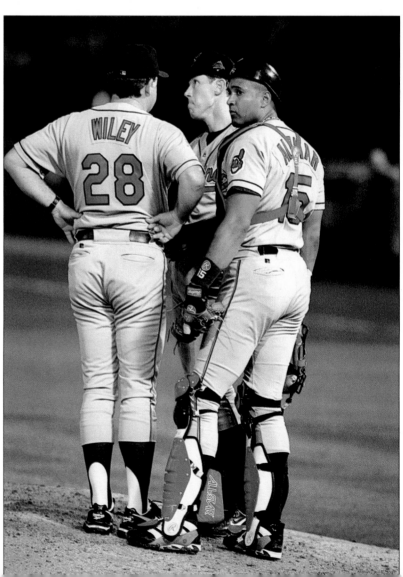

Manny Ramirez's solo homer in the fifth (opposite, top right) cut Cleveland's deficit to three. But Orel Hershiser gave up two runs in the fifth and left the game after one out (opposite bottom). In the sixth, Jim Thome's solo home run (bottom) was the last hit off Livan Hernandez.

Cleveland's Brian Giles tripled in the eighth (below) to drive home Marquis Grissom, but that was the last run the Tribe would score. Marlins bullpen ace Robb Nen (opposite) gave up two singles with one out in the ninth, and then struck out Jim Thome and Sandy Alomar to end the game.

"Robb's arm, I don't know where it comes from. It sure didn't come from me."
—Dick Nen, Robb's father

```
Cleveland  1 0 0  0 1 1  0 1 0 — 4
Florida    0 0 1  4 2 0  0 0 x — 7
Florida leads Series 1-0.
```

Miami, Florida   Oct. 19, 1997
GAME/JUEGO 2

"I think it's good for baseball because we get a chance to mix with different countries, learn different cultures. We learn a little meringue, a little salsa. Everybody comes together and has a good time."
—Charles Johnson

During warmups, Devon White (below) gets ready for the game, Livan Hernandez (right) signs autographs for fans, and Sandy Alomar (bottom) stands by the batting cage. Jim Leyland (opposite bottom) chats with Indians Pitching Coach Mark Wiley before the game.

"He's one of the top catchers in the game, offensively and defensively. It would be very difficult for us to have gone anywhere without Sandy Alomar."
—Mike Hargrove

Marlins ace Kevin Brown (opposite), who was 16-8 during the regular season, gave up six runs and 10 hits in six innings.

"Sometimes grounders find infielders, sometimes they find outfielders."
—Kevin Brown

Indians catcher Sandy Alomar Jr. just couldn't be stopped in 1997. The son of ex-Major Leaguer Sandy Alomar Sr. had a 30-game hitting streak during the regular season, an All-Star Game MVP Award and clutch hits throughout the playoffs. Alomar's key defensive play in the fourth—fielding a Charles Johnson sacrifice bunt in time to nail Moises Alou at third base—ignited the Indians as they went on to score five runs in the next two innings. Alomar also contributed a two-run homer in the 6-1 victory. Starter Chad Ogea, for whom the Tribe had not scored a run in his previous $19^{1}/_{3}$ innings of Post Season work, took the win as the Indians headed back home to the frigid north with the Series tied at a game apiece.

Cleveland's Chad Ogea (left) allowed just one run in his 6 $^2/_3$ innings for the win. He hit Gary Sheffield (right) with a pitch in the first inning. In the Marlins fifth, a Devon White single gets by Marquis Grissom (below). Florida's Edgar Renteria (opposite, below) had two hits, one a double, and scored a run.

"It's nice to know there are Gold Glovers behind me. You know you don't have to make the perfect pitch— just throw strikes and make them hit the ball."

—Chad Ogea

Moises Alou (above) is thrown out trying to move to third on an attempted sacrifice bunt by Charles Johnson in the fourth. Sandy Alomar (above) has a few words for Chad Ogea. Marquis Grissom (below) paced the Tribe with three hits, including an RBI single in the Indians three-run fifth.

Bip Roberts (top) dives back to first base. Matt Williams (bottom left) scores
one of his two runs. Bobby Bonilla (below) fields a grounder at third.

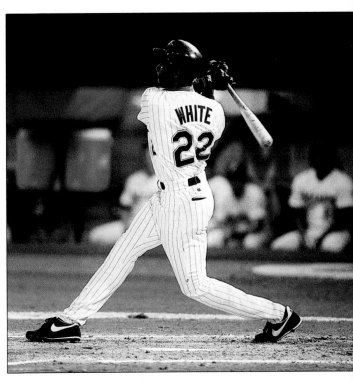

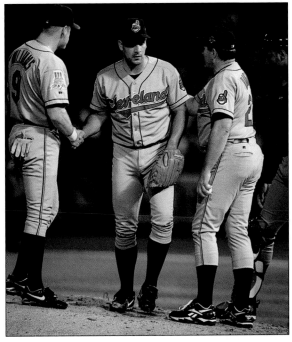

Sandy Alomar's two-run homer in the sixth (opposite) provided the Indians with a 6-1 lead. Tony Fernandez (top left) filled in for Bip Roberts and had two hits. So did Florida's Devon White (top right). Mike Jackson (right) held the Marlins scoreless in 1 $\frac{1}{3}$ innings of relief for Chad Ogea (above), who was saving his hits for later in the Series.

Antonio Alfonseca (right)
gave up three hits, but no
runs, in his two innings. He
helped himself with a double-
play grounder in the ninth, as
Tony Fernandez is forced at
second (below). Jose Mesa
(opposite, top) pitched a
scoreless ninth to send the
Series back to Cleveland tied
at one game each.

*"It's the manager's job to imagine
the worst, prepare to not let that
happen, and so even with a five-run
lead going into the 9th inning, I was
still very much afraid."*
—Mike Hargrove

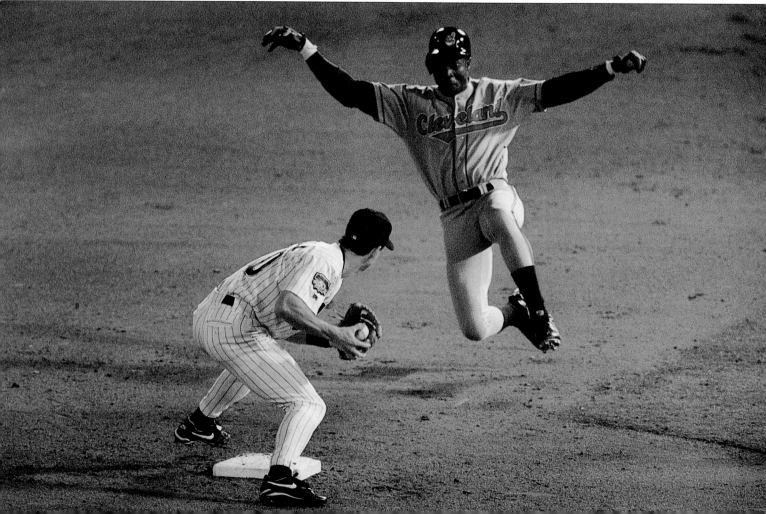

Cleveland	1 0 0 0 3 2 0 0 0 — 6
Florida	1 0 0 0 0 0 0 0 0 — 1

Series is tied 1-1

Cleveland, Ohio   Oct. 21, 1997

GAME/JUEGO 3

The weather was more suited for a long winter's night, but Cleveland was ready and excited to host its second World Series in the last three years.

"It would be like Picasso working with finger paints."
— Marlins coach Rich Donnelly on Jim Leyland and the designated hitter

On a wintry day in Cleveland, the Indians and Marlins combined for 17 walks and six errors in the second-highest scoring game in World Series history. Each team walked in a run, and three ninth-inning Indians errors allowed the Marlins to break open a 7-7 tie with a seven-run rally. Though the Tribe rallied back for four in their half of the ninth, they fell short in the 14-11 loss. Gary Sheffield hit his stride with five RBI, while Marquis Grissom's hit in his last at-bat made it 15 straight World Series games in which he had hit safely, surpassing Roberto Clemente for second on the all-time list.

Pitchers Charles Nagy (left) and Al Leiter (opposite, top) weren't factors in this more than four-hour slugfest that saw the teams combine for 25 runs and 26 hits. Gary Sheffield (bottom) hit his first Series home run in Game 3. "I feel this was my most clutch game as a Marlin," he would later say. Tony Fernandez's ninth inning error (opposite, botttom left and right) was one of three Indians miscues that led to seven Florida runs.

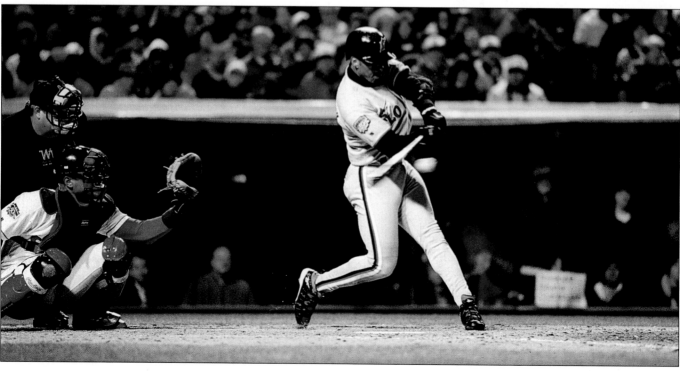

"The biggest problem with the cold is the slick feeling on the ball. The ball becomes like a cue ball."
—Al Leiter

"As long as the heart stays warm, you're all right."
—Jim Leyland

Darren Daulton's (opposite) fourth-inning homer was one of four in the game by both teams. Jim Thome (left, and above) poked his second home run of the Series, a two-run blast in the fifth. Marquis Grissom (top) had two hits which extended his World Series hitting streak to 15 consecutive games.

61

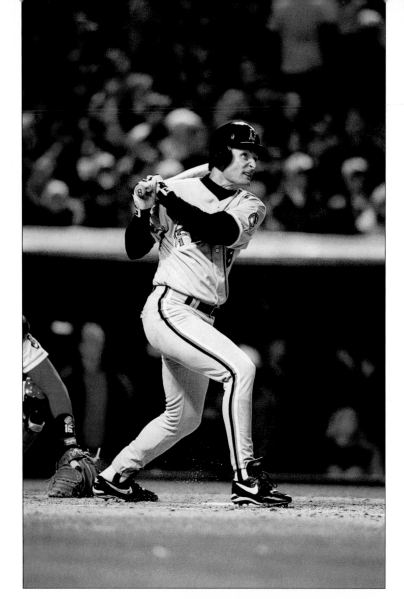

"I think the biggest play of the game was Eisenreich's home run. It gave us hope again."
—Gary Sheffield

Jim Eisenreich's two-run homer (opposite, top left and center right) in the sixth cut the Marlins' deficit to 7-5. Felix Heredia (opposite, right) relieved Al Leiter in the fifth and held the Indians scoreless for 2 $\frac{1}{3}$ innings. Bobby Bonilla (opposite, bottom) gets the out with a throw from his knees. Gary Sheffield (bottom) leaps to rob Jim Thome of a home run in the seventh.

Paul Assenmacher (right) was the only Indians pitcher not to allow a run in Game 3. Sandy Alomar (bottom left) goes after a pop foul. Edgar Renteria (bottom right) flags down a ground ball.

"Beware of broken bats" was a popular refrain in Game 3. It didn't help Devon White (top), who went hitless. Bobby Bonilla (left and above) led off the ninth with a walk and came around to score on Marquis Grissom's error. Bonilla's run was the first of seven for Florida in the inning.

Edgar Renteria (opposite, top left) tries to snag Jim Thome's one-out single in the ninth inning. Even with ace reliever Robb Nen (opposite, top right) pitching the ninth inning, Cleveland scored four times. Nen got Omar Vizquel to ground out to second to end the second-longest nine-inning game in World Series history.

Florida	1	0 1	1 0 2	2 0 7	—	14
Cleveland	2	0 0	3 2 0	0 0 4	—	11

Florida leads Series 2-1

"This is Jim Leyland's team. We owe it to him."
—Gary Sheffield

Cleveland, Ohio   Oct. 22, 1997
GAME/JUEGO 4

A winter wonderland in October came to Jacobs Field for Game 4. The Marlins, who take batting practice at home in shorts and T-shirts, have to wear more suitable apparel. The game-time temperature of 38 degrees was one of the coldest ever for a World Series game.

"Most clubs have the fifth-inning infield drag. Here, we've got the fifth-inning plow."
—Orel Hershiser

Snow flurries throughout the game gave Jacobs Field a surreal look, and the wind-chill factor had temperatures as low as the teens, but the offensive firepower of Matt Williams and Sandy Alomar kept the crowd warm and led the Indians to a 10-3 victory to even the Series at two games apiece. The matchup of rookie pitchers, 23-year-old Tony Saunders of the Marlins and Cleveland's 21-year-old Jaret Wright, was a World Series rarity.

Rookie Jaret Wright (opposite), son of ex-Major Leaguer Clyde Wright, pitched six strong innings in Game 4. Edgar Renteria's single in the first with one out (left) had no effect, because Bobby Bonilla grounded into an inning-ending double play. Rookie Tony Saunders (bottom), who made his Major League debut in May, gave up six runs in three innings.

Saunders (right) gave up three runs in the first, including a two-run shot from Manny Ramirez (below). Matt Williams (opposite top and bottom) scored three runs in the game, one in the first on Sandy Alomar's double and one in the third on Tony Fernandez's single.

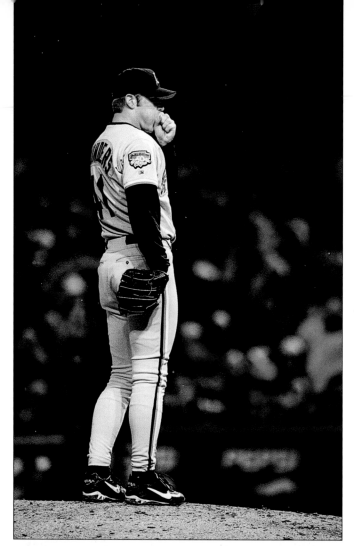

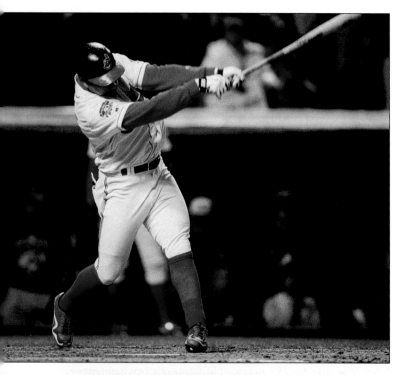

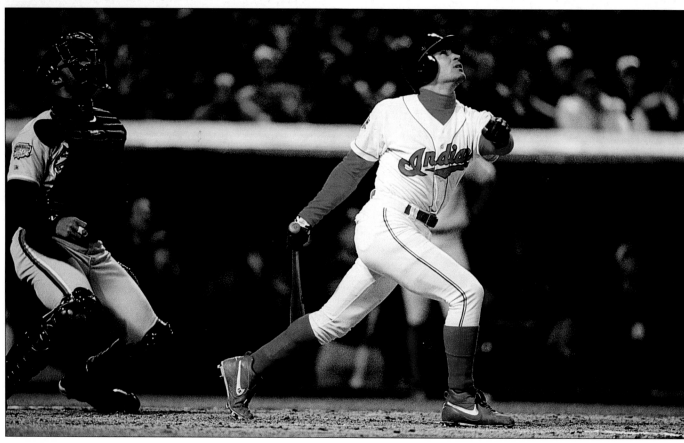

Sandy Alomar (opposite) had three hits and three RBI in Game 4. Craig Counsell (top left) steals second base in the third. Manny Ramirez (top right) scores on David Justice's infield single in the Indians half of the third. The Indians, including Sandy Alomar (above) were hot at the plate all night, pounding out 16 hits. The same can't be said for the Marlins, who had only six hits, or the umpires.

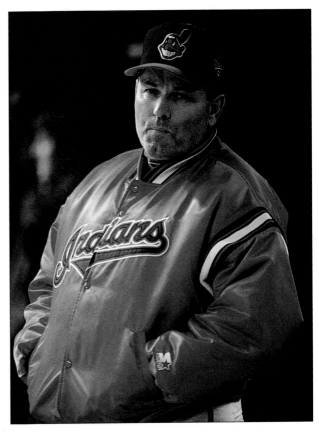

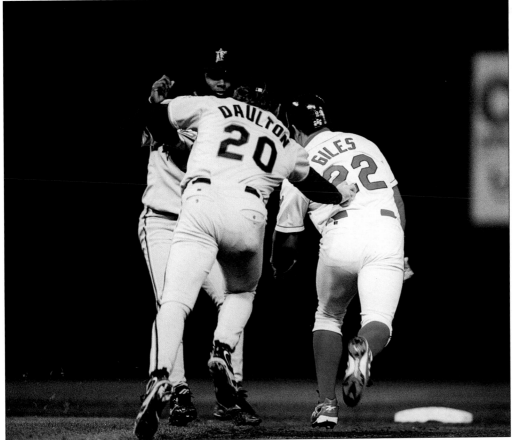

Jim Thome (opposite, bottom) shows great concentration as he goes after a foul ball late in the game. Moises Alou (top left) went deep in the sixth inning for his second homer of the Series. Mike Hargrove (above) shows the intensity of the Series. Brian Giles is picked off first after singling home Tony Fernandez in the seventh (left).

"Now everybody is in the same boat. We're back even and the Series comes down to the best of three."
—Sandy Alomar

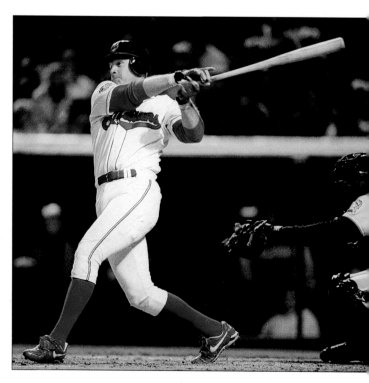

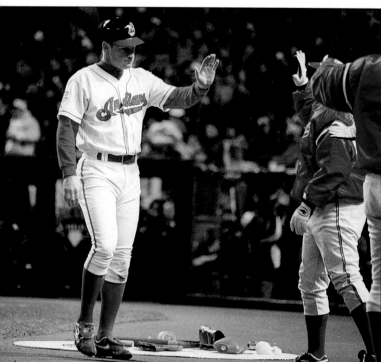

Jay Powell (top left) allowed two runs in the eighth on Matt Williams' first homer of the Series (top right and above). Jim Thome singled to center with two outs and was forced at second (right and opposite, top left) The Tribe's 10-3 win evened the Series at two games apiece.

Florida	0 0 0 1 0 2 0 0 0	— 3
Cleveland	3 0 3 0 0 1 1 2 x	— 10

Series is tied 2-2

Cleveland, Ohio   Oct. 23, 1997
GAME/JUEGO 5

It was the coldest game in World Series history, and one swing by Moises Alou ruined Cleveland's night. With the Indians up 4-2 after a steady six innings from Orel Hershiser, Alou's three-run home run put Florida ahead to stay. Despite a three-run rally by the Indians in the ninth, the Marlins held on for an 8-7 win and sent the Series back to Miami with a three-games-to-two lead. Alou finished the game 3-for-5 with four RBI. With his three-run homer in the third inning, Indians catcher Sandy Alomar set a record for RBI in a single Post Season with 19.

Florida Manager Jim Leyland (left) wanted to take a three-games-to-two advantage back to warm and sunny South Florida. His Marlins would have to face "Bulldog," Orel Hershiser (opposite, top) for the second time. Gary Sheffield (opposite, bottom) had two hits and scored one run in the game.

"The fans here are unbelievable. The 10th man thing, it's kind of true. Without them I don't know if we'd be where we are right now."

—Charles Nagy

Livan Hernandez, the eventual World Series MVP, earned his second World Series victory, despite walking eight and surrendering six runs, five earned. Omar Vizquel's sacrifice bunt (opposite, bottom) moved Bip Roberts to second in the first. The Marlins drew first blood in the second when Darren Daulton (left) led off with a double and scored on Charles Johnson's single (below). Craig Counsell (bottom) was thrown out at home trying to score on Devon White's double.

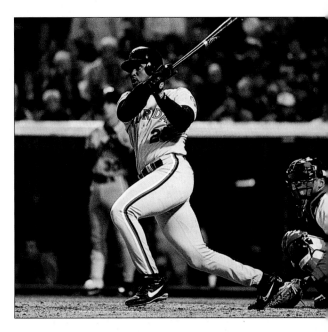

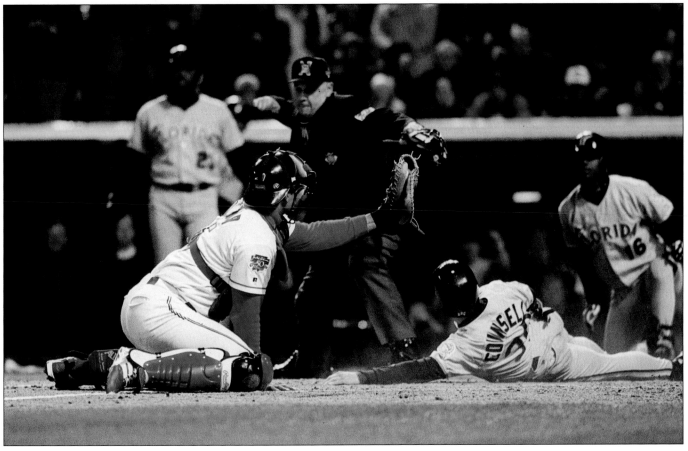

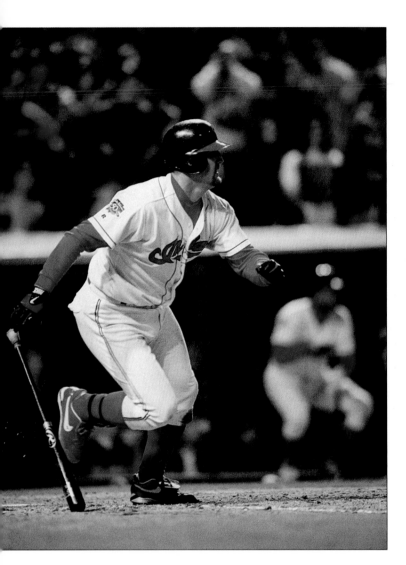

The Indians got to Livan Hernandez in the second as Jim Thome (left) tripled and scored on Sandy Alomar's single. Thome scored again in the third on Alomar's two-out, three-run homer (bottom left and right).

Cleveland's 4-2 lead lasted until the sixth when Moises Alou (left) homered with two on and two out. Jeff Conine (bottom left) and Charles Johnson followed Alou's blast with singles and ended Orel Hershiser's night (bottom right). Brian Giles did what he could do to track down the home run (right).

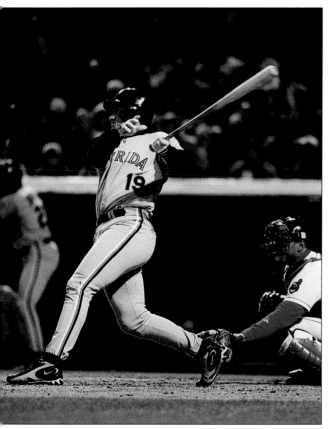

Orel Hershiser (below) was pulled after 5 $^2/_3$ innings. Jeff Juden (right) was the fourth pitcher used by the Tribe in the game. Manny Ramirez (bottom right) was forced out at second on a double-play grounder hit by David Justice in the seventh. Moises Alou led off the eighth with a single and stole second (opposite, top and bottom left). He eventually scored on Charles Johnson's single. Devon White (opposite, bottom right) doubled with two outs.

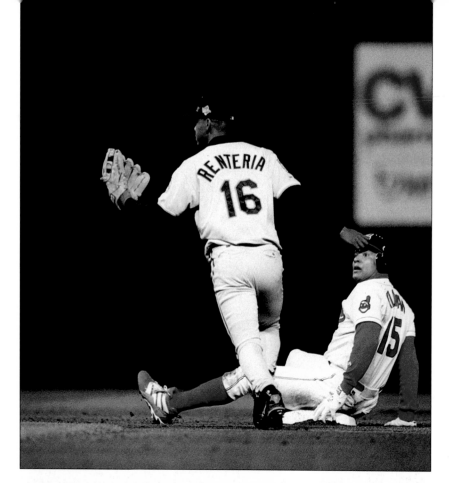

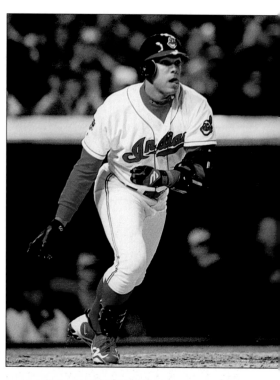

The veteran Bonilla (above) tried to settle down the rookie Hernandez, who left after eight innings (opposite, top left). In the top of the ninth, Jose Mesa (opposite, top right) allowed the run that ended up being the margin of victory for Florida. The Indians rallied for three runs in the bottom of the ninth with the help of David Justice's two-run single (top right). He was out at second (right) as Matt Williams grounded into a fielder's choice.

| Florida | 0 2 0 | 0 0 4 | 0 1 1 | —8 |
| Cleveland | 0 1 3 | 0 0 0 | 0 0 3 | —7 |

Florida leads Series 3-2

Miami, Florida   Oct. 25, 1997
GAME/JUEGO 6

Favorable weather conditions for the players—and the fans—of both teams were the order of the day as the 1997 World Series returned to South Florida.

"It was," said Marlins Manager Jim Leyland, "one of those games where you tip your hat to the other team." Cleveland's timely hitting and stellar defense earned them a 4-1 victory back in balmy Miami, forcing the first World Series Game 7 in six years. With two hits and two RBI from pitcher Chad Ogea, two run-scoring sacrifice flies from Manny Ramirez, great defense from a team that boasted six Gold Glovers, and a bullpen that pitched to perfection, the Indians set the stage for baseball's ultimate game. Marquis Grissom's Willie Mays-like basket catch in deep center on a Jeff Conine fly ball, and Omar Vizquel's deep-in-the-hole stop of a ground ball marked perhaps the two best defensive plays of the Series.

The Indians took a 2-0 lead in the second thanks to pitcher Chad Ogea's two-run single, scoring Matt Williams and a sliding Jim Thome (top). Ogea (opposite, bottom) and Kevin Brown (opposite, top) each pitched five innings, with Ogea getting the win. In the third, Omar Vizquel doubled, stole third (above, right) and scored the Indians third run off a Manny Ramirez sacrifice fly to deep left center.

Chad Ogea's two-run single to right field in the second (opposite, top left and right) proved to be the game-winning hit. Devon White (opposite, bottom) couldn't throw out Jim Thome, who was Ogea's second RBI. Ogea struck again in the fifth with a leadoff double. He took third (left) on a Bip Roberts single, and scored on Ramirez's sacrifice fly (bottom left). Roberts was picked off first to end the inning (below).

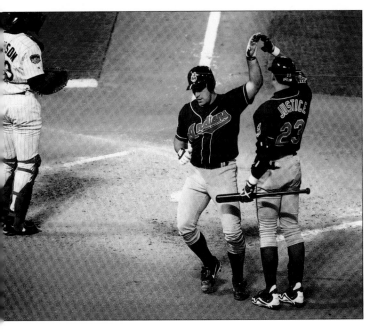

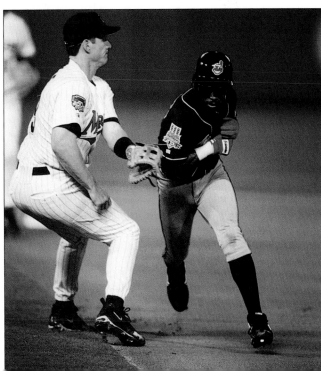

Moises Alou (top) and Charles Johnson (left) both singled to lead off the fifth. Alou ended up scoring Florida's lone run of the game. Felix Heredia (above) pitched two scoreless innings in relief of Kevin Brown. So did Mike Jackson (opposite, top left) in relief of Chad Ogea. Craig Counsell (opposite, bottom) led off the seventh with a single, but couldn't score.

In the eighth, Edgar Renteria (above) tries to complete a double play. After Matt Williams (top right) doubled to lead off the ninth, Ed Vosberg (right) came in and shut down the side, including pinch hitter Kevin Seitzer (opposite, top left). In the home half of the ninth, Devon White (opposite, top right) gave Marlins fans hope with a one-out triple. But Jose Mesa (opposite, bottom right) struck out Edgar Renteria and got Gary Sheffield to ground out, setting the stage for Game 7.

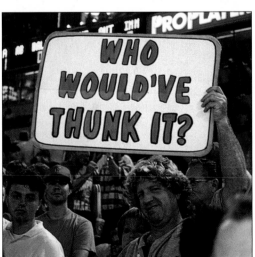

Cleveland 0 2 1 0 1 0 0 0 0 —4
Florida   0 0 0 0 1 0 0 0 0 —1
Series is tied 3-3

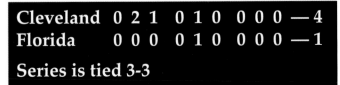

Miami, Florida   October 26, 1997
GAME/JUEGO 7

Among the Game 7 spectators: Orel Hershiser's former Dodgers manager, Hall of Famer Tommy Lasorda (bottom left); and Cleveland pitcher John Smiley (bottom right), who broke his left arm late in the season.

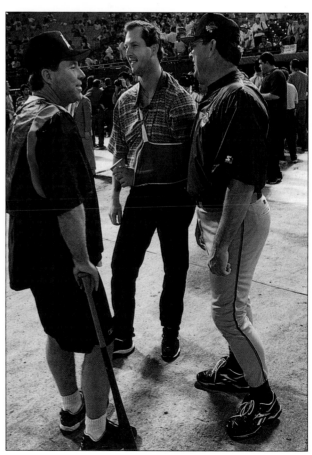

After more than a week of diplomacy by the U.S. Government, Miriam Carreras was finally allowed to leave her native Cuba to visit her son, Livan Hernandez, prior to Game 7.

Veteran Al Leiter (left) and rookie Jaret Wright (below) were chosen to start the biggest game of their careers.

"Most of the kids Jaret Wright went to school with are still trying to figure out what their college major will be. He's pitching the seventh game of the World Series."
—Bob Costas

There is perhaps no greater moment in professional sports than a Game 7 of the World Series. When that game goes into extra innings, as this one did, the edge-of-the-seat tension is gut-wrenching for even the coolest fan. After the Indians built an early 2-0 lead on a Tony Fernandez two-run single, and Bobby Bonilla's seventh-inning solo shot brought the Marlins to within one, the fate of the Series rested in the bullpens. The Marlins scored one in the bottom of the ninth to tie the game, and in the bottom of the 11th, with two out and the bases loaded, Edgar Renteria's hit squeaked through the middle. And the Florida Marlins won the World Series in just their fifth year of existence.

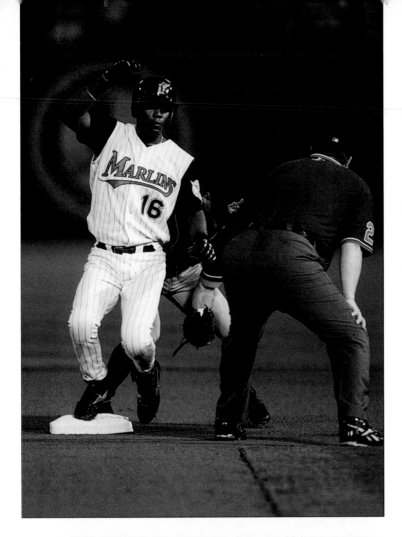

After Cleveland went down in order in the top of the first, Florida went on the attack in the bottom half with Edgar Renteria's double (left). After walking, Gary Sheffield was forced out (above) when Darren Daulton grounded into an inning-ending double play. The Tribe scored their only runs of the game in the third when Tony Fernandez (bottom left) singled home Jim Thome and Marquis Grissom (below).

A single from Alomar in the fourth (top left) and a stolen base from Vizquel in the fifth (above) couldn't produce any more runs for the Tribe. Dennis Cook (left), who didn't give up a run during the entire Series (3 $\frac{2}{3}$ innings pitched) kept it close by pitching a scoreless seventh for the Marlins.

Florida finally got to Jaret Wright when Bobby Bonilla (opposite) led off the seventh with a solo home run. Paul Assenmacher (top right) relieved Jaret Wright (top left) with one out in the seventh. Matt Williams (above) takes a breather as he watches Brian Anderson (right) in the eighth.

Cleveland tried to extend their lead in the ninth. Matt Williams (above) led off with a walk, but was forced out at second on a Sandy Alomar fielder's choice. After Florida Manager Jim Leyland pulled Antonio Alfonseca (top right) for Felix Heredia, Jim Thome (right) singled Alomar (opposite, top left) to third. Robb Nen (opposite, top right) finished the inning and kept the Tribe from scoring. Jose Mesa (opposite, bottom) was called on to stop the Marlins in the ninth.

"We showed tonight
that anyone who
thought these two
teams didn't belong in
the World Series was
full of garbage."
    —Sandy Alomar

Down by a run in the bottom of the ninth, Moises Alou (top left) led off with a single to center. After Charles Johnson's single moved Alou to third, Craig Counsell's sacrifice fly (below) brought home Alou with the tying run. Below, Cleveland Manager Mike Hargrove meets with his infield and battery.

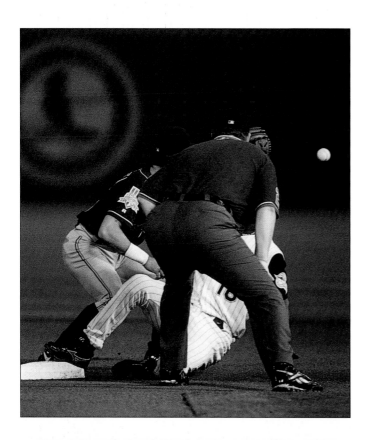

Florida threatened in the 10th as Edgar Renteria (top left and right) singled with one out and moved to second on Gary Sheffield's infield hit. But with two outs, Charles Nagy (left) got Moises Alou to fly out to shallow right field to end the threat.

"He threw me a slider for my first pitch, I took it for a strike. I knew he was going to throw me another slider and I hit it."
—Edgar Renteria

Orel Hershiser (top) started to warm up in the 11th, but never made it into the game. With two outs and the bases loaded, Edgar Renteria (below) singled home Craig Counsell, and the Marlins had won the 1997 World Series. Renteria was the Game 7 MVP.

Cleveland	0 0 2	0 0 0	0 0 0	0 0	—2
Florida	0 0 0	0 0 0	1 0 1	0 1	—3

Florida wins Series 4-3

"The Marlins are World Champions, and a 5-year-old child has become king."
—Marlins broadcaster Joe Angel

"I guess every little boy dreams of this. For me, I always thought it was a fantasy."
—Jim Leyland

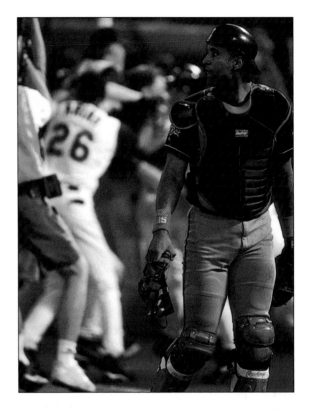

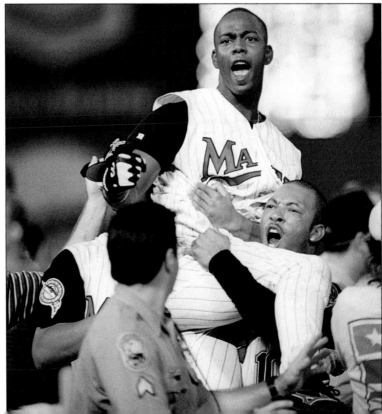

"This is when people find out what they're made of. Either you have the pain for life, or it goes away and you become stronger."
—Tony Fernandez

Jubilation on one side and reflection on the other were a charged counterpoint after Game 7. Livan Hernandez (opposite, bottom left) shows off his World Series Most Valuable Player Award, while Tony Fernandez (opposite, middle right), Sandy Alomar (opposite, bottom right), Mike Hargrove (top right), and Charles Nagy (middle right) answer the tough questions.

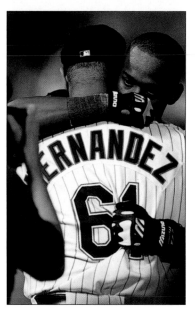

*"I dedicate this victory and this trophy to my mother. Everything is for her.
This victory is for Miami and all of Latin America. It belongs to all of you."*
     —Livan Hernandez

Two days later, the Marlins shared their triumph with all of South Florida during day-long celebrations. Livan Hernandez (opposite, bottom left) and Gary Sheffield (below) show their appreciation to the fans.

THE WORLD SERIES IN NUMBERS

World Series Records
Set in 1997

Most Strikeouts, One Inning
Edgar Renteria, FLA-2
Most Walks, Batters, 7 Game Series
40 Cleveland
Most Walks, Both Clubs, 7 Game Series
76
Youngest Pitcher to Win Opener
Livan Hernandez, FLA
22 years, 7 months, 28 days
Coldest Game Time Temperature
38 degrees, Game 4
Largest Attendance, 7 Game Series
403,617

World Series Records
Tied in 1997

Reaching Base Safely, 9 Inning Game
5, Matt Williams, CLE, Game 4 (11th time)
Consecutive Strikeouts
5, Devon White, FLA, Games 3-4 (seventh time)
Earned Runs Allowed, Pitcher, One Game
7, Orel Hershiser, CLE, Game 1 (sixth time)
Consecutive Base on Balls, Pitcher
3, Charles Nagy, CLE, Game3 (seventh time)
Most Base on Bal
Most Sacrifice Flies, Game
2, Manny Ramirez, CLE, Game 6 (second time)
Most Stolen Bases, Inning
2, Omar Vizquel, CLE, Game 7 (ninth time)
Most At-Bats, 7 Game Series
33, Devon White, FLA (fourth time)
Most Errors, One Inning
3, Cleveland, ninth inning, Game 3 (seventh time)
Sacrifice Flies, Game, Both Teams
3, Cleveland 2, Florida 1 (third time)
Consecutive Home Runs
Moises Alou and Charles Johnson, FLA, fourth inning, Game 1 (11th time)
Most Combined Pitchers Used, Nine Inning Game
11, Cleveland (7), Florida (4), Game 3 (third time)
Most Runs Scored, Single Team, Ninth Inning
7, Florida, Game 3 (second time)
Most Runs Scored, Both Teams, Single Inning
11, Florida (7), Cleveland (4), ninth inning, Game 3 (third time)
Homers In Both Leagues
Matt Williams, CLE, 10/27/89 with San Francisco vs. Oakland, Game 3 and 10/22/97 with Cleveland vs. Florida, Game 4 (seventh time)

GAME ONE

Cleveland	ab	r	h	bi
Roberts 2b	4	1	2	0
Vizquel ss	4	0	0	0
MRamirez rf	3	1	1	1
Justice lf	4	0	2	1
Williams 3b	5	0	1	0
Thome 1b	5	1	1	1
Alomar c	5	0	1	0
Grissom cf	3	1	2	0
Hershiser p	2	0	0	0
Juden p	0	0	0	0
Branson ph	1	0	0	0
Plunk p	0	0	0	0
Giles ph	1	0	1	1
Assenmacher p	0	0	0	0
Totals	37	4	11	4

Florida	ab	r	h	bi
White cf	4	0	0	0
Renteria ss	4	0	0	1
Sheffield rf	2	1	0	0
Bonilla 3b	3	2	2	0
Daulton 1b	2	1	1	0
Conine 1b	2	0	1	1
Alou lf	3	1	1	3
Johnson c	3	1	1	1
Counsell 2b	3	1	1	0
Hernandez p	2	0	0	0
Cook p	0	0	0	0
Powell p	0	0	0	0
Cangelosi ph	1	0	0	0
Nen p	0	0	0	0
Totals	29	7	7	6

Cleveland	1 0 0	0 1 1	0 1 0	—4
Florida	0 0 1	4 2 0	0 0 x	—7

E-Sheffield (1). DP-Cleveland 1. LOB-Cleveland 12, Florida 6. 2B-Roberts 2 (2), Counsell (1), Grissom (1), Giles (1). HR-Alou (1), Johnson (1), MRamirez (1), Thome (1). S-Vizquel, Hernandez.

Cleveland	IP	H	R	ER	BB	SO
Hershiser L (0-1)	4.1	6	7	7	4	2
Juden	.2	0	0	0	0	0
Plunk	2	1	0	0	1	1
Assenmacher	1	0	0	0	0	2

Florida	IP	H	R	ER	BB	SO
Hernandez W (1-0)	5.2	8	3	3	2	5
Cook	1.2	0	0	0	1	2
Powell	.2	1	1	1	2	1
Nen S (1)	1	2	0	0	0	2

WP-Juden

T-3:19. A-67,245. Umpires-HP, Montague; 1B, Ford; 2B, West; 3B, Kosc; LF, Marsh; RF, Kaiser.

GAME TWO

Cleveland	ab	r	h	bi
Roberts 2b	3	0	1	2
TFernandez ph-2b	2	0	2	0
Vizquel ss	4	1	2	0
MRamirez rf	5	0	0	0
Justice rf	3	0	1	1
Williams 3b	4	2	2	0
Thome 1b	4	0	1	0
Alomar c	4	2	2	2
Grissom cf	4	1	3	0
Ogea p	2	0	0	0
Jackson p	1	0	0	0
Mesa p	0	0	0	0
Totals	36	6	14	6

Florida	ab	r	h	bi
White cf	5	0	2	0
Renteria ss	4	1	2	0
Sheffield rf	2	0	0	0
Bonilla 3b	4	0	0	0
Conine 1b	3	0	1	1
Daulton 1b	1	0	0	0
Alou lf	4	0	2	0
Johnson c	3	0	0	0
Zaun ph	1	0	0	0
Counsell 2b	3	0	0	0
Brown p	2	0	0	0
Heredia p	0	0	0	0
Eisenreich ph	1	0	0	0
Alfonseca p	0	0	0	0
Floyd ph	1	0	0	0
Totals	34	1	8	1

Cleveland	1 0 0	0 3 2	0 0 0	—6
Florida	1 0 0	0 0 0	0 0 0	—1

DP-Cleveland 1, Florida 3. LOB-Cleveland 6, Florida 9. 2B-Vizquel (1), Renteria (1), Alou 2 (2), TFernandez (1), White (1). HR-Alomar (1). S-Ogea.

Cleveland	IP	H	R	ER	BB	SO
Ogea W (1-0)	6.2	7	1	1	1	4
Jackson	1.1	1	0	0	0	1
Mesa	1	0	0	0	1	1

Florida	IP	H	R	ER	BB	SO
Brown L (0-1)	6	10	6	6	2	4
Heredia	1	1	0	0	0	1
Alfonseca	2	3	0	0	0	0

HBP- by Ogea (Sheffield).

T-2:40. A-67,025. Umpires-HP, Ford; 1B, West; 2B, Kosc; 3B, Marsh; LF, Kaiser; RF, Montague.

GAME THREE

Florida	ab	r	h	bi	Cleveland	ab	r	h	bi
White cf	5	0	1	0	Roberts lf	5	1	1	2
Renteria ss	4	2	1	0	Vizquel ss	4	0	0	0
Sheffield rf	5	2	3	5	MRamirez rf	5	0	1	1
Bonilla 3b	5	1	1	2	Justice dh	3	2	0	0
Daulton 1b	4	3	2	1	Williams 3b	5	0	0	0
Conine 1b	0	0	0	0	Alomar c	3	2	2	1
Alou lf	5	0	0	0	Giles ph	0	1	0	0
Eisenreich dh	3	1	2	2	TFernandez 2b	4	0	1	1
Abbott ph-dh	1	0	0	0	Grissom cf	3	2	2	1
Floyd ph-dh	0	1	0	0	Nagy p	0	0	0	0
Johnson c	5	2	3	0	Anderson p	0	0	0	0
Counsell 2b	5	2	2	1	Jackson p	0	0	0	0
Leiter p	0	0	0	0	Assenmacher p	0	0	0	0
Heredia p	0	0	0	0	Plunk p	0	0	0	0
Cook p	0	0	0	0	Morman p	0	0	0	0
Nen p	0	0	0	0	Mesa p	0	0	0	0
Totals	42	14	16	12	Totals	36	11	10	10

Florida	1 0 1	1 0 2	2 0 7	—14
Cleveland	2 0 0	3 2 0	0 0 4	—11

E-Leiter (1), Bonilla 2 (2), Grissom (1), Thome (1), TFernandez (1). DP-Florida 1, Cleveland 2. LOB-Florida 9, Cleveland 9. 2B-Sheffield (1), Roberts (3). HR-Sheffield (1), Daulton (1), Thome (2), Eisenreich (1). S-Roberts. SF-TFernandez.

Florida	IP	H	R	ER	BB	SO
Leiter	4.2	6	7	4	6	3
Heredia	2.1	0	0	0	1	0
Cook W (1-0)	1	1	0	0	0	1
Nen	1	3	4	4	2	1

Cleveland	IP	H	R	ER	BB	SO
Nagy	6	6	5	5	4	5
Anderson	.1	1	1	1	0	0
Jackson	.2	2	1	1	1	0
Assenmacher	.2	3	0	0	0	1
Plunk L (0-1)	.2	2	4	3	2	1
Morman	.1	1	0	2	0	1
Mesa	.1	2	1	1	0	0

WP-Mesa

T-4:12. A-44,880. Umpires-HP, West; 1B, Kosc; 2B, Marsh; 3B, Kaiser; LF, Montague; RF, Ford.

FLORIDA MARLINS

PLAYER	AVG.	G	AB	R	H	TB	2B	3B	HR	RBI	BB	SO	SB	CS	SLG.	OBP	E
Abbott	.000	3	3	0	0	0	0	0	0	0	0	1	0	0	.000	.000	0
Alou	.321	7	28	6	9	20	2	0	3	9	3	5	1	0	.714	.387	0
Arias	.000	2	1	1	0	0	0	0	0	0	0	0	0	0	.000	.000	0
Bonilla	.207	7	29	5	6	10	1	0	1	3	3	5	0	0	.345	.281	2
Cangelosi	.333	3	3	0	1	1	0	0	0	0	0	2	0	0	.333	.333	0
Conine	.231	6	13	1	3	3	0	0	0	2	0	0	0	0	.231	.231	0
Counsell	.182	7	22	4	4	5	1	0	0	2	6	5	1	0	.227	.345	1
Daulton	.389	7	18	7	7	12	2	0	1	2	3	0	1	0	.667	.455	0
Eisenreich	.500	5	8	1	4	7	0	0	1	3	3	1	0	0	.875	.636	0
Floyd	.000	4	2	1	0	0	0	0	0	0	0	1	0	0	.000	.333	0
Johnson	.357	7	28	4	10	13	0	0	1	3	1	6	0	0	.464	.379	0
Renteria	.290	7	31	3	9	11	2	0	0	3	3	7	0	0	.355	.353	1
Sheffield	.292	7	24	4	7	11	1	0	1	5	8	5	0	0	.458	.485	1
Wehner	.000	0	0	0	0	0	0	0	0	0	0	0	0	0	.000	.000	0
White	.242	7	33	0	8	13	3	1	0	2	3	10	1	0	.394	.306	0
Zaun	.000	2	2	0	0	0	0	0	0	0	0	0	0	0	.000	.000	0
Brown	.000	2	3	0	0	0	0	0	0	0	0	0	0	0	.000	.000	0
Hernandez	.000	2	2	0	0	0	0	0	0	0	0	2	0	0	.000	.000	1
Leiter	.000	2	2	0	0	0	0	0	0	0	0	2	0	0	.000	.000	1
TOTALS	.272	7	250	37	68	106	12	1	8	34	36	48	4	0	.424	.363	8

PITCHER	G	GS	W	L	SV	ERA	Opp. Avg.	IP	H	R	ER	HR	BB	IBB	SO
Alfonseca	3	0	0	0	0	0.00	.250	6.1	6	0	0	0	1	0	5
Brown	2	2	0	2	0	8.18	.375	11	15	10	10	1	5	0	5
Cook	3	0	1	0	0	0.00	.091	3.2	1	0	0	0	1	0	5
Heredia	4	0	0	0	0	0.00	.111	5.1	2	0	0	0	1	0	5
Hernandez	2	2	2	0	0	5.27	.283	13.2	15	9	8	3	10	1	7
Leiter	2	2	0	0	0	5.06	.244	10.2	10	9	6	1	10	1	10
Nen	4	0	0	0	2	7.71	.381	4.2	8	5	4	0	2	0	7
Powell	4	0	1	0	0	7.36	.333	3.2	5	3	3	1	3	0	2
Saunders	1	1	0	1	0	27.00	.538	2	7	6	6	1	3	0	2
Vosberg	2	0	0	0	0	6.00	.273	3	3	2	2	0	3	1	2
TOTALS	7	7	4	3	2	5.48	.291	64	72	44	39	7	40	2	51

WP-Hernandez